What Readers are Saying

This book can be of service to many people. It can be used as a thorough fourth step of the 12-step programs for those who are not fortunate enough to be in one of the many recovery programs. For those of us who are, it is a very welcome adjunct for proving insights and keeping us on track. As a Life Coach, I will be using it as a tool for individual and group sessions. It will be a great framework for seminars.

Barbara Fredricks, BA, CPS.
Author: "Addictions and Family Healing."

Molly Nelson's book is a great resource for me. Her "List of Resentments" in chapter 3 helped me identify resentments I did not realize I had. They were buried deep within me. I have been healing my resentments for many years. Each resentment I heal blesses me with deeper feelings of being happy. I want as much happiness as possible and this book helps me do that. Thank you, Molly.

Robert Dunwoody,
CHT, MA, CRM, CAADAC

We all wish for that happy life, but what lies between living such a dream and the difficult reality we actually experience is what Molly Nelson bridges in an effective way.

The process she describes is very complete and worked well for me. She gives excellent descriptive examples that really help guide to explore feelings, fears, and resentments in depth. At the same time there is no negative judgment. She does not even hesitate to share from her own experience situations that were obviously an embarrassment to her at some time. With good humor she was able to go beyond it all, and her book offers ways for anyone to do the same. We all experience the shame of being judged by others and ourselves and wanting to crawl into a hole, but Molly Nelson is not holding back at all. I love the openness and the honesty she shares, and so gives courage to others to do the same.

This book is an excellent tool for anyone who wants to really make changes in his/her life. It is well organized, is perfectly guiding the reader with many examples, and then offers two effective ways to find the feelings, fears, and resentment. Finally, she offers opportunity to prepare for situations in the future that may bring old responses up, and how they would now be approached in a healthy way.

I'd say, "Well done, Molly Nelson, and thank you."

Maria Kingsley,
Ordained Ministerial Counselor,
Hypnotherapist, EFT & NLP Practitioner

Living Happily Ever After

Releasing Wounds, Hurts, and Resentments

A Workbook

Molly Nelson
2015

This workbook provides a process for releasing the wounds, hurts, and resentments that plague us throughout our lives.

Copyright © 2015 by Molly Nelson

All rights reserved.

Book design by Molly Nelson

The purchase of this material entitles the buyer to reproduce the List of Resentments and the worksheets for The Process and The Release for personal use only – not for commercial resale. Reproduction of these materials for group teaching is prohibited without prior written permission. No part of this book may be reproduced (except as noted above), stored in a retrieval system, or transmitted in any form or be any means (mechanically, electronically, recording, etc.) without the prior written consent of the author or publishing company. The only exception is by a reviewer who may quote short excerpts in a review.

Molly Nelson Books are available for order through
Ingram Press Catalogues

This book is a work of non-fiction. Names, characters, and incidents are either products of the author's imagination, or are used with permission or are used fictitiously. Although the author uses actual stories in some cases, they are only intended as examples to learn by.

Molly Nelson
Visit my website at www.LivingHappilyEverAfter.life

Printed in the United States of America
First Printing: January 2016
Published by Sojourn Publishing, LLC

ISBN: 978-1-62747-163-3
eBook ISBN: 978-1-62747-164-0

Acknowledgements

How can I ever thank enough Les Jones, Lecturer, University of Arizona, Department of English for the hours he spent editing this book. He made it more succinct, clear, and powerful than the original I handed him. Thank you 10 to the 23rd.

Barbara Fredricks who read the original draft, and whose enthusiasm sustained me through the revisions, thank you. Her insight as a former substance abuse counselor and currently as a Life Coach added immensely.

Tom Bird of Sojourn Publishing for his lectures, and retreats in How to Write a Book in a Weekend.

To Alan Hill, cousin extraordinaire, for his faith in the work and support in getting it up and running. Thank you.

Tom Puetz, who shared his story of the anguish he felt as a Vietnam draftee, combatant, and returning veteran, and for his very powerful poem. His book, "Secret Choices", eloquently gives words to the anguish veterans with PTSD can feel.

Jean Seagroves whose further editing gave me good lessons in grammar and particularly commas.

For those who have purchased eBook versions, you can download the List of Resentments and the Worksheets from my website:

www.LivingHappilyEverAfter.life.com

Table of Contents

Preface xi

Introduction xv

Chapter 1: The Nature of Our Fears 1

Chapter 2: Our Negative Characteristics 7

Chapter 3: The List of Resentments 11

Chapter 4: The Process 21

Chapter 5: The Release 27

Chapter 6: Examples of the Process and Release 37

Chapter 7: Conclusion 59

Bibliography 63

The Twelve Steps of Alcoholics Anonymous 65

Worksheets 67

Preface

I'm a happy person living a joy-filled life. On the outside it may look less than ideal; I use a walker. I consider my physical condition to be an inconvenience or a challenge, but I can walk and my walker can also function as a chair or a wheelbarrow. My blue healer service dog is a source of constant playfulness and laughter. It wasn't always this way as my story attests. However, I found a road out of wounds, hurts, and resentments that brought me to my present state. Let me take you down that road.

In 1965 I was miserable. I was so fat. Something had to be done. I weighed 230 pounds and I knew that if I just got thin I could be happy. My husband left because I was fat and depressed.

I had waged a battle with dieting starting at age ten. Sometimes I achieved a normal weight but I always gained back what I had lost and more.

Not only had I been a fat kid, but also, I often wet my pants. My classmates made hell for me and I resented the wounds and hurts I endured. I was always the last one chosen for a team and always ashamed and guilty. Why I could not control myself was completely beyond me. If I wasn't stuffing myself with food, my pants were wet. Sad, sad kid; angry, angry kid; resentment, resentment, resentment. My brother once asked my parents, "Why is she so mad at us?" Didn't they know they were supposed to make it all right? Didn't they know they were supposed to fix me? How I resented them.

My mom did try and she was very wise. She did not make a big deal out of my problems. When I was old enough, she made me wash out the soiled blanket that covered my rubber sheet. In this way, I learned that I was responsible for my life and would have to deal with the consequences of my handicaps. She also rushed me from Oregon to Ann Arbor, Michigan to see a famous urologist at the University of Michigan Medical School. After a dismal week in the hospital, he offered no diagnosis and to me this confirmed that my problems were incurable.

Later my mother sought out other help for me. This was in the days of Freud. Diagnosis: Penis envy. I did envy my older brothers who had more privileges. They stayed up later and went to more places, but were those reasons to want a penis?

Finally at age 14, I was diagnosed with Hunner's ulcers or interstitial cystitis, an ulcerative condition of the bladder, cause unknown. Throughout my life I have tried many cures, pills, and treatments, but with very little benefit. Eventually, the bed-wetting stopped but I still have incontinent accidents during the day.

As a teenager, my weight was a bigger bugaboo. Through dieting and sports – golf, tennis and swimming, I finally achieved a normal size through most of my twenties. After college graduation, I began teaching first grade. I met my future husband and started to gain weight. I lost it all for my wedding day, but after our marriage, I yo-yoed up and down.

For a wedding present, I told my husband that I would support him through completing his Ph.D. I got a teaching job in Berkeley during the early 60's in a de-facto racially segregated school. Some of the children had much anger from the living conditions produced by prejudice that made their poverty or situations so stressful that they brought with them anger and acted out in school. This resulted in stress that I covered up by over-eating.

During the second year at Berkley, I became pregnant but lost the baby in the third trimester. The OB doctor told my husband that I should view it as a delayed menstrual period. Apparently, the MD did not know that conception and implantation of the egg produce all sorts of hormones that go crazy when the pregnancy terminates. I didn't know that either and could not explain the deep depression that I plunged into.

At the end of my husband's course work, he announced that with a doctorate he deserved a better wife. This threw me into an even deeper depression. I developed a mantra, "I wish I were thin I wish I were dead". I did a half-hearted attempt at suicide but my husband took the razor out on my hand.

I later came to the idea that I was a "scholarship wife". In lieu of a scholarship, you married a teacher or a nurse.

As my marriage was dissolving, my mother insisted that I see a psychiatrist; she found one for me. I took to my first visit a list of all the things that were wrong with me plus a letter from my husband about his perception of what was wrong with me. The psychiatrist responded by asking, "What's right with you?" I was astonished. The only thing I could think of was that I had a sense of humor.

After the divorce, I started to rebuild my wounded self with more help from the psychiatrist. Dieting and exercise gave me an acceptable body. More self-discovery through therapy and reading gave me a better self-image. But then I lost the acceptable body.

Eventually I found the 12-step program – Overeaters Anonymous – where my journey to inner peace, self-acceptance, and happiness accelerated. It was doing a fourth step, "Made a fearless and searching moral inventory," that I began to look deeper into myself. Phyllis G conducted a workshop on the fourth step using an extensive list of possible resentments, page after page of them. I had much to write on many of them. Of 150 on one list, I related to 85. It took months just to write them all out.

As I worked resolving the resentments and listened to others' struggles at meetings, I began to be more self-accepting and soon my family noticed that I was becoming much more loving. I also felt closer to friends than ever before. These feelings were joyful; I realized that my friends found something in me to love and so I could love me too. Could it be that my negative and judgmental thinking had come to an end? Was self-acceptance and understanding making me a happier person?

The original fourth step process was to write out each resentment, adding what my role was in creating it and what were the negative characteristics (thoughts and behaviors) I needed to work on. Over the years, I have found other ways to enhance the process that has led me to greater understanding, self-acceptance, and self- love.

Am I perfect? No, I am a work in progress. But at least I catch an unloving thought before it takes control of me, and I have ways of turning it around. Will I ever be through with this journey? No. The 10th step of the 12- step program is "Continue to take personal inventory and when we were wrong, promptly admitted it".

With less blaming of others for the choices I've made, I can take ownership of who I am. Whatever my weight is – up, down, or sideways – I am so much happier and accepting of others just the way they are, and most importantly, I am accepting of me just the way I am. I do not have to carry around the heavy burden of wounds, hurts or resentments.

This book grew from the lists of resentments from the fourth step workshop. It was the mirror in which I could look at myself and eventually see myself and others with love, acceptance, and compassion. I offer this to you so you might find that wonderful, loveable, glorious person you are.

Introduction

Happiness is a quality and way of life that we seek by desperately looking outside ourselves. However, it actually resides within as a kind of merry song that keeps playing in the background. It is "the sound as of some joyous elf, singing sweet songs to please himself." (Edna St. Vincent-Millay)

To find our song is more an act of cleansing than of composition. The song is muffled and muted by the discord of thoughts and feelings that we've picked up from family, school, the media, and others; in short all those who ask, "How do you measure up?" Then tell us, "You're not rich, thin, tall, smart, or cool enough."

Our family tells us to be someone they can be proud of, or conversely, they tell us that we will never amount to much. Our childhood may have had name calling that led to wounds, hurts, and resentments that we still carry with us.

Resentment – or re-sent anger – is an expression of inner unhappiness. Turned outward it goads us into abusing our loved ones and friends. Turned inward it leads to depression and despair. Resentments can stifle us from moving forward or from participating fully in life.

We have been told we couldn't change the past. But can we? Since the past lives only in our memory, can we change our memory? Can we choose to see our past differently? Yes, but with work!

The work is enlightening because it makes us "lighten up". Resolving my resentments, I have found, though, is like walking through a briar patch. Inner journey work is thorny. Bringing up old hurts so they can finally be released can be painful. It's like popping a boil; it hurts for a second but then true healing can take place. Getting these "infections" out will bring about the healing and the happiness we deserve. It's the greatest gift we can give ourselves and, we are the only ones who can.

Someone said that the predominant emotion of animals in the wild is fear, but the predominant emotion of humans is resentment – the anger we continue to carry into the future.

What exactly is anger? Actually, it is the companion of our instinct fear. The two, fear and anger, travel together somewhat like a medieval knight with his ever faithful squire. "Make way for Sir Fear," shouts the loyal Squire Anger.

Fear alerts us to dangers, particularly two: (1) we will lose something we have or (2) we won't get something we want. We can then summon anger to use its power and energy to get what we want or keep what we have. Have you ever seen a child throw a temper tantrum in a toy store? He has learned that anger is a powerful "getter".

Anger and resentment can also result from three other fears: fear of rejection or abandonment, fear of loss of control, and fear of inadequacy or failure. We have to get rid of these circular, painful, and fearful thoughts if we want to live happily. There are certain steps we must take to see how our fears drive us. Living joyfully is the result of cleansing the past and it is a process.

In the next few chapters, I will lead you on the path to freeing yourself from resentment:

1. You must go through the lists (see Chapter 3) and check the resentments that pertain to you.
2. Take each item and apply The Process (see Chapter 4).
3. Then complete The Release, letting go of hurtful events (see Chapter 5).

Doing this work may be hard, but it is like ridding yourself of a constricting garment. You will breathe more freely, I promise.

Deep down, underneath our resentments, lurk our negative thoughts, behaviors and characteristics. The famous Seven Deadly Sins plus two are the nine monsters we try to cover up: theft, pride, greed, gluttony, envy, jealousy, anger, and I would add lust and victimhood. They are the burning coals that fuel our anger.

Perhaps you are wondering why you must go through so much to change. Do you know the story of the butterfly and the scientist who studied it?

As he held a cocoon in his hand, the scientist noticed that the critter inside was struggling to get out. He thought he would help by slitting the case with a scissors. Alas, the poor butterfly died. It needed to struggle against the sides of the case to get the blood flowing throughout its body.

Likewise, we need to work to get off the cocoons formed by our wounds, hurts, and resentments so we too can become empowered to fly. May you soar on your flight to a joyous life.

A word about confidentiality: If you live with other people, it is wise to keep this work locked away. You may be in a situation where people in your life might misuse their knowledge of your past mistakes to start destructive fights or "blackmail" you in a variety of ways. To avoid this some people write in code or use initials. If you're writing on a computer, you can keep your files on a thumb drive which you can store somewhere away from prying eyes.

Keeping on with the work can be challenging. If you are in a 12-step or other self-recovery program, working with a sponsor, a counselor or a coach can keep you climbing up and out of the pit of pain that the memories may bring.

Chapter 1
The Nature of Our Fears

"Fear leads you directly into the path of what you fear."
Anonymous

Fears are the underlying drivers of resentments. Some fears are based on physical danger; others are culturally learned. Our physical fears are usually of pain or death: fear of falling off a cliff, fear of being killed, fear of a needle at the doctor's office. These fears are outside the realm of this book. What concern us are the fears that fuel resentments.

They include: (1) fear of rejection/abandonment, (2) fear of loss of control, (3) fear of inadequacy/failure, (4) fear of not getting something we want, (5) fear of losing something we have.

These fears are the buried drivers in our minds, choosing what roads we take, and therefore what lies ahead. Getting rid of our fears is a process of discovery that teaches us who we are at our core, and what is secretly driving us. The process starts with looking at our wounds, hurts, and resentments. I'll lump these three words together and call them "resentment."

Our fears can intermingle with our resentments. For example, resentment over rejection/abandonment is often coupled with fear of inadequacy/failure. Rejection is a barometer of our feelings of inadequacy. An adequate or successful person is not going to dwell on feelings of rejection, but one who feels inadequate or a failure is.

The fear of rejection is akin to the fear of losing control. We hear people being put down for not being in control of their spouses, kids, emotions, appearance, or weight.

Fear of Rejection/Abandonment

This is an instinctual fear because as social animals with long childhoods we need protecting. As children, we require grownups to fill our needs. We fear that we will be abandoned. We know deep within that we cannot survive alone. Listen to the howls of babies who are left by their mothers even shortly. Our very survival depends on group membership.

We find ourselves tied to relationships because (1) our partner or spouse cannot get along without us, (2) we cannot get along without them, (3) the time is just not right to leave and (4) they would not allow it, etc. In short, we stay in destructive relationships so we will not be alone.

Fear of rejection can frighten us into being nice even to our abusers. We become the people pleasers who knock ourselves out for family, friends, bosses, etc., and then resent that we are not appreciated enough. This pattern can start when we are children trying to please our parents or avoid punishment.

One time when I was dieting strenuously, I asked my family to help me prepare healthy meals; if they would cook the potatoes and make a salad, I would prepare the entrée when I got home from a 60-minute rush-hour commute. Yet every night neither the potatoes nor the salad was ready. I fumed while I got the whole dinner ready. When we sat down, I did not raise the issue. Early on, I learned to keep my mouth shut or they might not be happy. It did not occur to me to <u>not</u> fix the potatoes or salad, and just do my part. Instead I fumed, not daring or even knowing how to ask that my needs be filled for fear of upsetting the apple cart. How many times have we stayed in a dysfunctional relationship to not displease someone else?

Fear of abandonment is another facet of rejection. What if a person leaves us? How will we get our needs met? Anyone who has gone through the death of a spouse or a divorce knows the panic of suddenly not having someone to wash the clothes, change the oil in the car, be a presence in the house, or give structure to our lives.

Our whole "team player" ethic means that acceptance is vital. In early human history, banishment was a death sentence. In some societies, being shunned is tantamount to being killed.

Fear of Losing Control

Loss of control is another great fear. If we take on the responsibility and control for every task, than we can smother the people around us. Giving up control is a fear frequently felt by parents. There are real dangers out there that we would not want our children to experience, yet we also need to give them the freedom to learn from their mistakes. This becomes a balancing act. Knowing when to ease up on controls is one of the great tasks of parents, as anyone raising a teenager knows. One mother put it succinctly, "God, grant me the serenity to back off."

When we assume control, we write scripts for other people to follow: We become the father who wants his son to follow in his footsteps, the husband who wants his wife to be prettier or the wife who wants the husband to be richer. Or even me who wanted my family to cook part of our meals.

When I was living with my brother, he would drive us to the store taking a route longer than the one I preferred. I told him about the shorter route, but he went the other way. It took me a while to figure out the obvious: that it didn't really matter which way we went as long as it got us there. It also took me a while to learn that if someone is driving, they have their hands on the steering wheel, and that will determine which way the car will go.

I felt that if I could just get others to follow my directions, I could stay in control, and I could predict what would happen in my less than predictable world. When they didn't, I felt resentful.

If I lost control of myself – such as bursting out in tears – I would suffer shame or ridicule. "Why aren't you more controlled?" Always being in control was a huge task, as I grew up with bladder incontinence. I resented myself for not being in control.

Fear of Inadequacy/Failure

Loss of control can go hand in hand with fear of inadequacy. How will I look to other people? Am I okay? What if they find out I don't know everything? If I lose control of the situation, will they think I'm dumb? I once heard someone disparage a man because he did not have control over his wife; this led him to wonder if he was an inadequate male.

Resentment against school is common. How did you feel with red marks on your spelling paper? How did you rank with the other guys or girls? Being chosen last? If you failed to win the gold medal, did you tell yourself "I'm nothing"? These examples all invoke the fear of inadequacy and failure.

Fear of inadequacy/failure is at the core of our self-doubts, our "terminal lack of enoughness" – the gnawing feeling that we're not thin enough, rich enough, tall enough, good enough, etc. These are coupled with the thought, "If only I were better," which anguishes our souls and brings resentment of those perpetrators who point out our flaws.

Chapter 2
Our Negative Characteristics

"Every man is a moon, and has his dark side
which he never shows to anybody."
Mark Twain

Negative characteristics, defects of character, seven deadly sins, etc., are the hidden bugaboos that contaminate our souls. They are the "sins" that keep us bound in destructive behavior towards others, or more damaging towards ourselves. They are the attitudes and behavior that keep us from meeting life with exuberance and from seeing and experiencing life's possibilities, from living joyfully. They are also the basis of many resentments.

The original 12-step inventories began with the Seven Deadly Sins: theft, pride, greed, gluttony, envy, jealousy, and anger. I've combined several for simplification: greed/gluttony, envy/jealousy, and anger/resentment. I've also added lust and victimhood.

Pride is a sticky one, it comes in two forms. One is "toxic" pride, which leads us to elevate ourselves above all others. "Good" pride is being happy about an accomplishment. Toxic pride leads to war. Good pride leads to self-love.

Acting as a victim is a prevalent characteristic in our society. Bad things do happen to good people. Yet we need to accept it and take our power back. Bad things also keeps us thinking "poor me", a victim and is an attitude much less than joyful. If we stay in victim mode, we will even attract perpetrators. We are easy prey.

We can also be the perpetrator in our own lives by holding onto guilt, shame, and regret. These come from wishing we had made other decisions. We must realize that these choices were the best we could have made given <u>that we were the people we were then</u>. For instance, I regret that I was not a slender kid. Second helpings at dinner helped me cover up the pain I was experiencing at school. We are not the same people today that we were when the incidents took place that we now feel guilt, shame or regret. We learn by making mistakes. They are "GDLES": <u>G</u>ol <u>D</u>arn <u>L</u>earning <u>E</u>xperiences. One of the wisest words I've found is "Oops".

Chapter 3
The List of Resentments

"No man is angry that feels not himself hurt."
Sir Frances Bacon.

Put a 1 next to the items that upset you the most, a 2 for the lesser ones, and a 3 for the least if some emotion is still attached. Some of the items won't pertain to you – they will to someone else.

I have resentment because of (the):

___A close relationship
___Abstinent people
___Abuse by a parent
___Accumulating stuff
___Achievers
___Advertisements
___Age
___Aggressive people
___An alcoholic
___An addict
___Anger display
___Authority Figures
___Being afraid to look stupid
___Being afraid to stand up for my rights
___Being consumed by self
___Being a giver, not a taker
___Being or living with a pack rat
___Being a people pleaser
___Being a savior/rescuer
___Being asked, "Am I that fat, ugly, etc.
___Being a victim
___Being worse than you
___Being concerned about other's feelings
___Being embarrassed by others
___Being fat
___Being in a place I don't want to be
___Being intimidated
___Being late
___Being left alone
___Being left out
___Being not enough

___Being overlooked
___Being picky
___Being scared of anger
___Being second
___Being shy, self-conscious
___Being taken for granted
___Being talked down to
___Being teased
___Being told how/what to feel
___Being told how to live
___Being under the influence of a person
___Being under the influence of a substance
___Being unorganized
___Being what someone else wanted me to be
___Big appetite
___Binges
___Blaming others
___Bluffing
___Busy work
___Buying
___Can't accept criticism
___Can't accept failure (me or other)
___Cars, jewelry, travel
___Changes
___Character assassination
___Clothes
___Collecting grievances
___Commitments
___Communicators
___Comparisons

13

Chapter 3

___Competition
___Competitive situations
___Complainers
___Compulsive buying
___Condemning
___Conforming
___Confrontation
___Contempt prior to investigation
___Control
___Conversation
___Cover-ups
___Cravings
___Criticism
___Cultural programming
___Dead people
___Death
___Denied fear
___Denying ability
___Denying pleasure
___Denying sexuality
___Dependence on me
___Dependence on others
___Depriving others of love
___Depriving self of love
___Diets
___Disappointments
___Disciplined people
___Dishonesty
___Disloyalty to employers
___Do-gooders
___Doing other things than responsibilities
___Don't touch me attitude
___Drug companies
___Easy getters
___Effort or money spent on appearance
___Embroidering the truth

___Enabling
___Endangering our health
___Everybody who is better off
___Ex-spouse's new spouse
___Excuses for not being perfect
___Expectations
___Expecting perfection in self or others
___Extra time demanded by employer
___False humility
___Family
___Family relationships
___Fantasies
___Fast weight losers
___"Fat" doctors
___Father
___Favoritism
___Fear of my feelings
___Fears
___Feeling unworthy
___Femaleness or maleness
___Financial insecurity
___Food
___Former spouse
___Frustration
___Getting a job
___God
___Go-for-ing
___Good communicators
___Good health
___Good housekeepers
___Gossip
___Grandiosity
___Great bodies
___Grievance collectors
___Guilt producer
___Happiness with self
___Happiness with family

___Harboring resentments
___Having "less than" feelings
___Having to admit powerlessness
___Having to accept
___Having to accept those who don't accept me
___Having to ask for help
___Having to tell the truth about myself
___Health
___Hiding food from others
___Hiding vulnerability
___Higher status workers
___Holding on to guilt or resentment
___Homes
___Housecleaning
___Humiliation
___I don't know who I am
___I'll do it and everything else
___Illness
___Inability to do things
___In laws
___"In" group
___"In" people
___Inability to communicate
___Income tax
___Inconsiderate people
___Ingratiating behavior
___Instability in others
___Instant judgments
___Insurance
___Intellect
___Interruptive people
___Intolerance
___Intruding into my privacy
___"It was nothing" attitude
___Jealousies
___Job applications, resumes

___Knowledge
___Lack of accepting or giving apologies
___Lack of dependence
___Lack of honesty
___Lack of independence
___Lack of organization
___Laziness
___Lawyers
___Learned from angry parent
___Little eaters
___Living up to shoulds
___Love
___Lying
___Making excuses for self
___Male chauvinism
___Male/female validation
___Manipulating people
___Manipulation
___Married people
___Material things
___Medical profession
___Memories
___Men
___Men don't cry attitude
___Men's privileges
___Misdirected anger
___Missed communication
___Mistreatment of animals
___Mistreatment of the environment
___Mistreatment of people
___Moderate people
___Money managers
___Mother
___Mother's old tapes
___My body
___My boss
___My feelings discounted

Chapter 3

___My food
___My hobby
___My illness
___My program
___My projections
___My shortcomings
___My things
___My things taken
___My time schedule
___Name brands
___Need for other's validation
___Need for recognition
___Need for relationship(s)
___Need for status
___Need for time
___Need for unqualified acceptance
___Need to be somebody
___Needing others
___Negative reactions
___Never being satisfied
___Newcomers
___Not showing emotion
___Nobody did anything for me
___Non response to my anger
___Not answering letters/emails/phone calls
___Not asking for help
___Not able to express thoughts
___Not able to say no
___Not able to say yes
___Not able to set boundaries
___Not able to share
___Not appreciated
___Not being understood
___Not buying necessities
___Not concentrating
___Not delivering

___Not expressing feelings
___Not feeling until it grows
___Not fulfilling expectations
___Not getting help
___Not giving credit to another
___Not giving service
___Not having fun
___Not in control
___Not knowing how to change
___Not knowing who I am
___Not letting go of people'
___Not listening to others
___Not sharing
___Not sharing self
___Not taking criticism
___Not taking risks
___Not trusting
___Not wanting to go places
___Obsession
___Old feelings
___Old timers
___One-upmanship
___Optimists
___Organized religion
___Other people not taking my needs or me seriously
___Other people's messes
___Other's abilities
___Other's over-eating, drinking, or using
___Others laughing at me
___Other's pay rate
___Other's talent, ability, or education
___Other's time schedules
___Others shortcomings
___Overachiever
___Overdoing

___Over involvement
___Paranoid thinking
___Peer pressure
___People who are tolerant
___People who are intolerant
___People who are successful
___People pleasing
___People up on things
___People who are ok with themselves
___People who can drink without getting drunk
___People who can eat everything and not gain weight.
___People who do …
___People who do not understand me
___People who enjoy exercising
___People who express themselves clearly
___People who get attention
___People who get away with it
___People who get boy or girlfriends
___People who gorge on my binge foods
___People who have good clothes
___People who have their lives together
___People who indulge
___People who lose weight fast
___People who participate
___People who steal my ideas
___People who try to fix others
___People who were not attracted to me
___People with great jobs
___People with more money
___Perfectionists
___Performers without stage fright
___Phony leadership
___Physical problems
___Physical symptoms

___Picking "in" friends
___Politicians
___Poor me
___Popular people
___Position
___Power
___Power of words
___Practical Jokers
___Practicing compulsions
___Preparation for entertaining
___Price gougers
___Procrastination
___Professional training
___Projection vs. planning
___Proving yourself
___Punishment
___Putting self down
___Quitters
___Relatives' time
___Responsibilities
___Restrictions
___Right job
___Right love affair
___Right schools
___Risk takers
___Saboteurs
___Sagging skin
___Salad bars/smorgasbord
___Sales people
___Scheming or plotting
___Serene people
___Self-pity
___Self-sacrificing
___Setting me or others up
___Sexual greed
___Showcasing faults
___Sibling

Chapter 3

___Single people
___Sloppy appearance
___Smugness or self-righteousness
___Snobbery
___Sober, abstinent or "clean" people
___Somebody's interest
___Something is missing
___Spouse
___Standing on ceremony
___Staying hidden
___Stealing
___Stealing communication
___Stealing from family
___Stealing from self
___Stealing from stores
___Stealing love
___Stealing things
___Stealing trust
___Strong-willed controllers
___Structure in my life
___Stubbornness
___Stupidity in others
___Stupidity in self
___Substance abuse counselors
___Subtle manipulators
___Superior attitude
___Swearing/vulgarity
___Symbolic victories
___Take charge people
___Takers
___Taking the bigger piece
___Talent/ability
___Talented people
___Tangibles
___The baby sitter
___The perfect gift
___The skinny world

___The sober world
___The system (s)
___Thin or fat people
___Things I would like to be
___Things to do
___Those who don't show emotions
___Those who show emotion
___Time limits
___Time managers
___Tiredness
___Title
___To have without earning
___Treatment of old people
___Treatment of race
___Treatment of women
___Trying to evoke sympathy
___TV
___TV commercials
___Unable to express feelings at the time
___Unable to stay sober, clean, or abstinent
___Unfaithful lover
___Used as a weapon
___Waiting for people
___Wanting others to envy me
___Wanting to be the center of everyone's universe
___Watching TV
___Weakness
___Wearing masks
___Weather
___We can't say no
___What will others say
___When a friend got a lover
___Who can handle confrontation
___Who can say no
___Who don't have problems

18

___Who have energy
___Women
___Won't do demeaning jobs
___Work
___Workaholic
___Your partner's dependence
___Your partner's independence
___Youth

___Youth cult
Other resentments not on this list.
___
___
___
___
___

In the addendum, you will find forms that you can copy that will take you through The Process and The Release of these resentments. The following two chapters explain both.

Chapter 4
The Process

"The unexamined life is not worth living."
Socrates

The Process and Release are the two steps that will liberate you from the unhappiness. Read this chapter and the next to get a total picture of the work ahead of you. At first you may feel overwhelmed, but as you progress it will go faster and faster. Remember: How do you eat an elephant? One bite at a time. How do you write a book? One sentence at a time. How do you do The Process? One resentment at a time.

I would suggest that you do not more than two resentments at a time. As you progress, you can pick up speed, particularly as you see patterns emerge.

Look at The Process form. *Note:* There are two versions you can use: one is a narrative form; the other is a chart form. Pick the one that you are most comfortable with. Take a quick look-see at the forms below and then read the explanation of each section that follows.

The Process
Narrative Style

1. I RESENT _____ BECAUSE: The circumstance or situation.

2. EFFECTS: Self-esteem, security, personal relationships, sex.

3. WHAT WAS MY PART IN IT? WHERE WAS I AT FAULT?

4. FEELINGS: anger, fear, sad, shame, humiliation, guilt, pride, panic, depression, jealousy, indignation, inadequate/failure, defiance, apprehension, anguish, self-pity.

5. NEGATIVE CHARACTERISTICS: fear, anger, pride, lust, sloth, envy, greed, selfish, dishonest, self-seeking, blame, victim, theft.

6. WHICH FEAR: loss of control, rejection, inadequacy/failure, won't get something I want, or will lose something I have.

Chapter 4

The Process
Chart form

1. RESENTMENT: The circumstance or situation.	
2. EFFECTS: self-esteem, security, personal relationships, sex, ambition.	
3. WHAT WAS YOUR PART IN IT? WHERE WAS I AT FAULT?	
4. FEELINGS: anger, fear, sad, shame, humiliation, guilt, pride, panic, depression, jealousy, indignation, inadequacy/failure, defiance, apprehension, anguish, self-pity.	
5. NEGATIVE CHARACTERISTICS: fear, anger, pride, lust, sloth, envy, greed, selfish, dishonest, self-seeking, blame, victim, theft.	
6. WHICH FEAR: loss of control, rejection, inadequacy/failure, won't get something I want, will lose something I have.	

Living Happily Ever After

RESENTMENTS. This is the circumstance or situation. From the List of Resentments in Chapter 3 prioritize those you have starting with 1 the most hurtful, 2 the next most harmful, or 3 the ones that still cause you some ill feeling. Write each resentment on a separate worksheet. Later on as you work the Process, you will find that many of the 2s and 3s seem to evaporate. They may have been part of a 1 and after a while, they will have lost their sting. Perhaps you checked off two items that are so close that you can do one process that covers both: BOGO. (Buy One Get One)

EFFECTS: How does a resentment you checked affect your self-esteem, security, personal relationships, love life, ambition, etc?

WHAT WAS MY PART IN IT? What did I do that caused each situation or circumstance that led to the resentment? This can be a toughie. None of us wants to admit we were at fault, yet to know and accept ourselves we need to look at our blemishes.

FEELINGS: What feelings did/do you experience? Here is short list of responses: anger, fear, sadness, shame, humiliation, guilt, pride, panic, depression, jealousy, grief, inadequacy, failure, defiance, apprehension, anguish, self-pity, lust, etc. Add any more you can come up with. I came up with "sneaky-sly". It was a delicious feeling but not wholly honorable.

NEGATIVE CHARACTERISTICS: These are the underlying thoughts that are the basis of our characters or our personalities. How do you react to life? Easy going? Anxious? Angry? The negative ones provide the fuel for our resentments. For instance, you may be stung by a bee and be angry at the bee, though most of the time you are happy-go-lucky. However, if you walk through life angry and fault-finding about everything and the main tone of your conversation is "ain't it awful", then this is the negative characteristic that will allow you to spend the rest of your life hating bees.

NEGATIVE CHARACTERISTICS include: theft, pride, victim, greed/gluttony, envy/jealousy, anger/resentment, grief, victim, and lust. There are probably a lot more but this will be enough to get you started on looking beneath the surface at yourself.

Although we use the same words for NEGATIVE CHARACTERISTICS as FEELINGS they differ in that feelings are more on the surface of our consciousness, but the NEGATIVE CHARACTERISTICS are the hidden drivers deep down that you may be unaware of — and yet is your basic reaction to life. Your goal is to recognize them and change the ones that are holding you back. For instance, is greed/gluttony keeping you in some kind of squirrel cage demanding more and more stuff as you push yourself to exhaustion needing more and more stuff?

<u>WHICH FEAR:</u> What were you afraid of that led to the original anger? Rejection, loss of control, inadequacy/failure, that you won't get something you want, or that you will lose something you have.

In the example below, I use the narrative format. My answers are italicized.

RESENTMENT: *My husband wanted a divorce.*

EFFECTS: *self-esteem, security, love life, personal relationships (who gets which friends).*

MY PART IN IT: *I became very overweight and depressed.*

FEELINGS: *guilt, shame, sadness, indignation, failure, humiliation, self-pity*

NEGATIVE CHARACTERISTICS: Which of these are the main culprits of my personality? *Greed/gluttony are the main ones. I could not get enough food to stop the torrent of anger and anguish inside. Self-pity with its sidekick, hopelessness was also there along with humiliation, which is a twisted form of pride.*

WHICH FEAR: *rejection, loss of control, inadequacy/ failure, I'll lose something I have.*

Chapter 5
The Release

"The most powerful agent of growth and transformation is something much more basic than technique: a change of heart."
John Welwood

Congratulations. Getting through THE PROCESS takes the most work. The last part is to release the person or event that caused your resentment. This step came later in my life, after I had finished the original fourth step. I needed to understand the other person's point of view and where they were coming from in order to get more clarity.

The Release Narrative Form

1. I SEE THAT _____ DID THE BEST _____ COULD GIVEN THE PLACE THAT _____ WAS/WERE IN.

2. DESCRIBE THEIR POINT OF VIEW.

3. LIST THE GOOD TRAITS THIS PERSON OR INSTITUTION HAD.

4. I FREELY AND FULLY FORGIVE _____ TO THE BEST OF MY ABILITY.

5. I CUT _____ LOOSE AND SET _____ FREE. NOW THEY ARE FREE AND I AM FREE.

6. I APOLOGIZE FOR THE PAIN I MAY HAVE CAUSED _____

7. I BLESS (WISH GOOD FOR) _____ .

8. THE GIFT OR THE LESSON I LEARNED WAS:

9. VISUALIZATION:

10. AFFIRMATION:

11. THE NEXT TIME THIS SITUATION COMES UP I WILL:

Chapter 5

The Release Chart Form

1. I SEE THAT ___ DID THE BEST ___ COULD GIVEN THE PLACE THAT ___ WAS IN.	
2. DESCRIBE ___ POINT OF VIEW.	
3. LIST THE GOOD TRAITS THIS PERSON OR INSTITUTION HAD.	
4. I FREELY AND FULLY FORGIVE ___ TO THE BEST OF MY ABILITY.	
5. I CUT ___ LOOSE AND SET ___ FREE. NOW ___ IS FREE AND I AM FREE.	
6. I BLESS (WISH GOOD FOR) ___.	
7. I APOLOGIZE FOR THE PAIN I CAUSED.	
8. THE GIFT or THE LESSON I LEARNED WAS:	
9. VISUALIZATION.	
10. AFFIRMATION.	
11. THE NEXT TIME THIS HAPPENS I WILL:	

1. <u>I SEE THAT</u>   <u>DID THE BEST</u>   <u>COULD GIVEN THE PLACE THAT</u>   <u>WAS/WERE IN.</u> This was the way that person or situation was. "That that is, is. That that is not, is not. Is that it? It is." (Alan Cohen)

This wise saying helps us to accept life and situations as they are. Fill in the blank on this section with how your think that person perceived the situation.

EX. *My husband was unable to cure my over-eating or my depression. He thought he had to fix me, but couldn't.*

2. <u>DESCRIBE THEIR POINT OF VIEW.</u> <u>WHERE WERE THEY COMING FROM?</u> What was their viewpoint? Children of alcoholic fathers frequently resent their mothers for not stopping the chaos. However, most people do not have the skills for dealing with an alcoholic situation. Was the husband the source of the family income? Did the wife believe she could not support the family without him? Did she believe in "for better or worse till death do us part?"

EX. *A successful man in our culture is defined as having an attractive wife and lots of money. This is the way my husband chose to be seen. From my husband's point of view, he had neither.*

3. <u>LIST THE GOOD TRAITS THIS PERSON OR INSTITUTION HAD.</u> My husband was a good father, fixer-upper, teacher, and loved to travel.

4. <u>I FREELY AND FULLY FORGIVE</u>   <u>TO THE BEST OF MY ABILITY.</u> This is the most liberating step <u>for you</u>. Forgiveness does not mean you condone the person. It means that you have let them be who they are. Forgiveness has been defined as UNCONDITIONAL ACCEPTANCE. This is the way they were—not the way you wanted them to be but simply how they were.

Forgiveness can be a hurdle that is difficult to jump over. In the development of our moral character, the first stage is "Don't get caught". Some people are stuck there. Anything is okay for them to do as long as they aren't caught. Child molesters are at this level. They also use threats and other coercions to keep their victim quiet. How do you avoid them – self-centered people and sociopaths – all those that have no concern for the other? Seek and listen to the opinions of trusted friends and family. Children are particularly vulnerable since they have not had experience to learn who not to trust. This makes them appealing to predators.

Chapter 5

Life coaches and EFT (Emotional Freedom Technique Practitioners) have been beneficial for helping victims free themselves of the trauma and unhealthy thoughts about themselves that continue to fuel the resentment.

The final stage of moral character development is the "social contract, "do unto others as you would have them do unto you." As you forgive, you hope others will forgive you for your lapses.

EX.: *I freely and fully forgive my husband to the best of my ability since this was the way he was.*

You may add some self-forgiveness:

EX. *I freely and fully forgive myself to the best of my ability since this is the way I was. I was raised to not express anger. Depression is anger turned inward pointing to powerlessness. Yet these negative feelings were driving my obsessive-compulsive eating.*

5. <u>I CUT   LOOSE AND SET   FREE NOW   ARE FREE AND I AM FREE.</u> The person involved in your resentment may still be a part of your life, but as you see them clearly, you can release your expectations of how they ought to be.

EX: *I cut my husband loose from my heart and set him free. Now he is free and I am free.*

I did two exercises, because I was so resentful. They were not gentle or loving but removed the bitterness and fury. I visualized my husband standing on the edge of a cliff and I pushed him over the edge gleefully, many times. I also visualized him lying on a rock while I took a sword and furiously chopped him up into little bits, again and again, many times. These exercises served to release the anger that was under the hopelessness and despair. Another technique is to use a soft bat and beat a pillow. These techniques help us to take back the powerfulness that we may have felt was taken from us.

6. <u>I BLESS (WISH GOOD FOR)   </u>. We get back what we put out. You want good in your life so put that out for them. The famous Hawaiian prayer/therapy is, "I'm sorry. Please forgive me. I love you. Thank you." The "thank you" is for the

opportunity to find the lesson in all this. This prayer/therapy has been shown to heal even violent situations

   EX: *I bless him and wish him well. May he have all the success and happiness he wants.*

7. <u>I APOLOGIZE FOR THE PAIN I MAY HAVE CAUSED</u>_____. The pain for them is that you did not accept their viewpoint. Not being understood hurts.

   EX: *I regret and apologize that I was not the attractive vibrant woman that I was when we were married.*

8. <u>THE GIFT OR THE LESSON I LEARNED WAS:</u>
Though getting to forgiveness is a giant step, there is something even more freeing, and that is recognizing The Gift or Lesson. With all the emotion attached to our resentments, the gift can be the growth that we can recognize and use.

   EX: *The gift was the motivation to do the self-exploratory work through psychotherapy, counseling and 12-step programs that made me a person that I could love and appreciate.*

   Wayne Dyer tells the story that his father abandoned the family which sent them into poverty. Wayne spent years in foster homes. However, he learned as a young boy that he could make money by running errands, raking leaves, shoveling snow, etc. He has always been able to make money. This was The Gift he received from his father.
   Out of adversity, we can learn skills to overcome our circumstances. We have within us great powers that only need to be developed. It can be through our trials that we are challenged to exceed ourselves and discover our power.
   Anne was raised by an alcoholic mother who was emotionally and physically abusive. To get away, Anne built herself a little refuge in the woods near her home where she could escape into books. She read everything in the public library. She became a brilliant student in school who skipped two grades and won scholarships to exclusive schools and a prestigious university.
   Her Gift was her love of reading which stretched her innate intelligence. To this day, she can read and absorb three or four books in a week. In the Information Age, that is a gift.

Chapter 5

9. <u>VISUALIZATION</u>. This can take two forms. The first is to see yourself released from your pain. How would you be, think, and behave without your lingering resentments? The second is to visualize how you want your life to look in the future.

> EX: *I saw myself out in the woods enjoying the smell of pine and the twittering of birds, enjoying life.*
>
> *Second, I saw myself slender, with my head high, walking and smiling. I also visualized my slender self as I looked in the past and kept the picture where I could recall it.*

10. <u>AFFIRMATION:</u>. Affirmations are positive thoughts that support visualization. They are said over and over until the new thoughts stick. People frequently write them on sticky notes and place them on the bathroom mirror. Others wear a bracelet, and each time an old negative thought comes up they say the affirmation and move the bracelet to the other wrist. Eventually they note that the bracelet stayed on the first wrist for a day. It takes what it takes, folks.

> EX. *I put up a sticky on the mirror, "My body is slender and strong. I stick to my food plan."*

11. <u>THE NEXT TIME THIS SITUATION COMES UP I WILL:</u> Life has a way of sending us lessons. If we don't learn them the first time, they will come back again, perhaps in another form. Some people marry abusers repeatedly.

> EX: *The next time I'm attracted to someone, I will confirm that his behavior matches his words. Moreover, I will listen to the assessment of trusted friends.*

A woman was having difficulty ending a love affair. She just could not get the right words together. So she called a friend and asked for help. He told her exactly what to say, and she wrote it down on a card then practiced it. Next she taped the card near her phone, so when the call came from the soon-to-be-former lover she was prepared. It worked.

You might want to tape these affirmations where you can see and repeat them frequently:

- I'm sorry. Please forgive me. I love you. Thank you.

- I can release the past and forgive everyone.
- I free everyone and myself in my life from old hurts. They are free and I am free to move into new glorious experiences.

Chapter 6
Examples of the Process and Release

"Experience is not what happens to a man.
It is what a man does with what happens to him."
Aldous Huxley

The Process: Betty. Sibling Rivalry

1. RESENTMENT: The circumstance or situation. HIGHLIGHTING FAULTS BY PUTTING SELF DOWN.	Betty speaks: I resented that my siblings pointed out so many things wrong with me. I was always admitting my faults, always showing others how bad I was. I was the worst kid on the block.
2. EFFECTS: self-esteem, security, personal relationships, sex, ambition.	Self-esteem, I'm so bad. Personal relationships: I wanted others to feel sorry for me or to deny that I was this bad.
3. WHAT WAS YOUR PART IN IT? WHERE WAS I AT FAULT?	I exaggerated my conditions and situations.
4. FEELINGS: anger, fear, sad, shame, humiliation, guilt, pride, panic, depression, jealousy/envy, indignation, inadequate/failure, defiance, apprehension, anguish, self-pity.	Shame and humiliation, Feelings of inadequacy, failure, anguish. Fear that if I don't point out my inadequacy, others will. Pride in being the worst one in the room. Self-pity.
5. NEGATIVE CHARACTERISTICS: fear, anger, pride, lust, sloth, envy, greed, selfish, dishonest, self-seeking, blame, and victim, theft.	Self-seeking for attention, acceptance, and sympathy. Victim (poor me).
6. WHICH FEAR: loss of control, rejection, inadequacy/failure, won't get something I want, will lose something I have.	Fear of rejection.

Chapter 6

The Release: Betty

1. I SEE THAT ___ DID THE BEST ___ COULD GIVEN THE PLACE THAT ___ WAS IN.	Betty: I did the best I could given that my older sibs constantly pointed out all my faults.
2. DESCRIBE ___ POINT OF VIEW.	If we don't point out Betty's faults, she won't be a family member we can be proud of.
3. LIST THE GOOD TRAITS THIS PERSON OR INSTITUTION HAD.	They wanted me to be accepted as an attractive person. They taught me to dance and how to apply make-up. Sometimes they helped me with my homework.
4. I FREELY AND FULLY FORGIVE ___ TO THE BEST OF MY ABILITY.	I freely and completely forgive my sibs – they wanted to make me socially acceptable. I forgive myself for not questioning their assessments.
5. I CUT ___ LOOSE AND SET ___ FREE. NOW ___ FREE AND I AM FREE.	I cut loose and set my sibs free. I cut loose from negative thoughts about myself.
6. I BLESS (WISH GOOD FOR) ___.	I bless my sibs and wish good for them, as I want good for myself.
7. I APOLOGIZE FOR THE PAIN I CAUSED.	I apologize for the negative remarks I made to my friends and for the damage I did to myself.
8. THE GIFT or THE LESSON I LEARNED WAS:	Keeping my thoughts positive. If I goof up, I can fix it without making a great to – do.
9. VISUALIZATION.	I see myself smiling and giving a high five for my accomplishments
10. AFFIRMATION.	I do good work and I am proud of it.
11. THE NEXT TIME THIS SITUATION COMES UP I WILL:	I will catch myself and think of a better way to do what I have criticized myself for. I can make mistakes since that's how we learn.

The Process: Brian. Packrat

1. RESENTMENT: The circumstance or situation: *ACCUMULATING THINGS.*	Brian speaks: I resented that I never had enough. I was never satisfied. I wanted more or better.
2. EFFECTS: self-esteem, security, personal relationships, sex, ambition.	Self-esteem: I have to have the most and the best.
3. WHAT WAS MY PART IN IT? WHERE WAS I AT FAULT?	I have to feel I'm better than the next guy.
4. FEELINGS: anger, fear, sad, shame, humiliation, guilt, pride, panic, depression, jealousy, indignation, inadequacy/failure, defiance, apprehension, anguish, self-pity.	Fear, shame, inadequacy, pride.
5. NEGATIVE CHARACTERISTICS: fear, anger, pride, lust, sloth, envy, greed, selfish, dishonest, self-seeking, blame, victim, theft.	Greed, pride.
6. WHICH FEAR: loss of control, rejection, inadequacy/failure, won't get something I want, will lose something I have.	Inadequacy. I won't get something I want.

Chapter 6

The Release: Brian

1. I SEE THAT ___ DID THE BEST ___ COULD GIVEN THE PLACE THAT ___ WAS IN.	Brian: I see that I did the best I could, given that I believed that "a winner is the one with the most toys."
2. DESCRIBE ___ POINT OF VIEW.	The more you have the better you are. People will respect you more. These are the trophies of success.
3. LIST THE GOOD TRAITS THIS PERSON OR INSTITUTION HAD.	I am willing to change myself and grow into a person I can appreciate. I'm finding value in simply being rather than having things.
4. I FREELY AND FULLY FORGIVE ___ TO THE BEST OF MY ABILITY.	I forgive myself for thinking my self-worth is based on possessions.
5. I CUT ___ LOOSE AND SET ___ FREE. NOW ___ IS FREE AND I AM FREE.	I can cut loose of "stuff" and still be pleased with who I am. I don't need other people's admiration.
6. I BLESS (WISH GOOD FOR) ___.	I bless the "stuff" that made me feel good, and for the good feelings that it brought at the time.
7. I APOLOGIZE FOR THE PAIN I CAUSED.	I apologize for spending on myself rather than sharing more with my family.
8. THE GIFT or THE LESSON I LEARNED WAS:	Stuff does not make me the person I want to be nor give me the happiness I've longed for. I wanted validation that I was successful.
9. VISUALIZATION.	I am with family and friends enjoying the moment of togetherness.
10. AFFIRMATION.	I am a loving, caring husband and dad.
11. THE NEXT TIME THIS SITUATION COMES UP I WILL:	I can look at a new "toy", appreciate it, and not have to own it.

The Process: Joan. Compulsive Buying

1. RESENTMENT: The circumstance or situation. *COMPULSIVE BUYING*.	Joan speaks: I resented that I could not stop buying, even things I did not need. I was a shopaholic.
2. EFFECTS: Self-esteem, security, personal relationships, sex, ambition.	It affects my personal relationships. My house was so cluttered my family was ashamed to bring people over.
3. WHAT WAS MY PART IN IT? WHERE WAS I AT FAULT?	I wanted more and more to fill up this feeling of emptiness. I did not explore why I felt so empty.
4. Feelings: anger, fear, sad, shame, humiliation, guilt, pride, panic, depression, jealousy, indignation, inadequacy/failure, defiance, apprehension, anguish, self-pity.	Inadequacy. Shopping filled up the emptiness and the feeling I was not enough.
5. Negative Characteristics: fear, anger, pride, lust, sloth, envy, greed, selfish, dishonest, self-seeking, blame, victim, theft.	Greed, I can't get enough.
6. WHICH FEAR: loss of control, rejection, inadequacy/failure, won't get something I want, will lose something I have.	I won't get something I want.

Chapter 6

The Release: Joan

1. I SEE THAT ___ DID THE BEST ___ COULD GIVEN THE PLACE THAT ___ WAS IN.	Joan: I see that I did the best I could to fill my empty feelings.
2. DESCRIBE ___ POINT OF VIEW.	Nothing would make me feel as happy as shopping.
3. LIST THE GOOD TRAITS THIS PERSON OR INSTITUTION HAD.	There were all these things in such abundance. Some were very beautiful. Even though I don't need that kind of lift now, I'm glad shopping was there when I needed it.
4. I FREELY AND FULLY FORGIVE ___ TO THE BEST OF MY ABILITY.	I freely and fully forgive myself to the best of my ability.
5. I CUT ___ LOOSE AND SET ___ FREE. NOW ___ IS FREE AND I AM FREE.	I cut loose from buying for pleasure instead of necessity. Now I am free.
6. I BLESS (WISH GOOD FOR) ___.	I bless myself and wish only good for me.
7. I APOLOGIZE FOR THE PAIN I CAUSED.	I apologize for the pain I caused my family by over-spending.
8. THE GIFT or THE LESSON I LEARNED WAS:	Spiritual nourishment can replace stuff and fill the emptiness. I learned to feel gratitude for what I have. I also learned to sell the "stuff" on EBay.
9. VISUALIZATION.	I imagined my house uncluttered and neat.
10. AFFIRMATION.	I buy only what I need, and have space for.
11. THE NEXT TIME THIS SITUATION COMES UP I WILL:	The next time I'm tempted to buy what is not on my shopping list, I will hold the item for a few moments in order to satisfy my urge to possess and then put it back.

The Process: Janice. Envy

1. RESENTMENT: The circumstance or situation: ENVIOUS OF POPULAR PERSON.	Janice speaks: I resented popular people. "I could be popular too if I went around being nice to everybody", I used to say as I watched Tricia go by surrounded by friends.
2. EFFECTS: Self-esteem, security, personal or sexual relationships, sex, ambition.	My self-esteem was battered as I wondered why Tricia was popular and I wasn't. "What's wrong with me?"
3. WHAT WAS MY PART IN IT? WHERE WAS I AT FAULT?	I came to realize that I used put-downs when I talked about others.
4. FEELINGS: anger, fear, sad, shame, humiliation, guilt, pride, panic, depression, jealousy, indignation, inadequate/failure, defiance, apprehension, anguish, envy, self-pity.	Anger that I was not popular. Envy of the popular ones. Sadness that I felt so alone. Shame that there must be something wrong with me. Inadequacy that I was not enough.
5. Negative Characteristics: fear, anger, pride, lust, sloth, envy, greed, selfish, dishonest, self-seeking, blame, victim, theft.	Envy, Self-seeking. Looking for acceptance and validation from others.
6. WHICH FEAR: loss of control, rejection, inadequacy/failure, won't get something I want, will lose something I have.	Rejection. Inadequacy (what's wrong with me?) I won't get something I want.

Chapter 6

The Release: Janice Envy

1. I SEE THAT ___ DID THE BEST ___ COULD GIVEN THE PLACE THAT ___ WAS IN.	Janice speaks: Tricia is naturally nice and friendly.
2. DESCRIBE ___ POINT OF VIEW.	Tricia likes people and knows how to get along with them. She sees the good in them.
3. LIST THE GOOD TRAITS THIS PERSON OR INSTITUTION HAD.	She was such a good role model for how to be friendly. I learned a lot from her.
4. I FREELY AND FULLY FORGIVE ___ TO THE BEST OF MY ABILITY.	There is no need to forgive Tricia. There is a need to forgive me for not understanding my pain.
5. I CUT ___ LOOSE AND SET ___ FREE. NOW ___ IS FREE AND I AM FREE.	
6. I BLESS (WISH GOOD FOR) ___.	I wish her well. She was not trying to hurt me.
7. I APOLOGIZE FOR THE PAIN I CAUSED.	I apologize for any mean things I said about her.
8. THE GIFT or THE LESSON I LEARNED WAS:	If I look at what's good about another person or tell them something I see good about them, I will have more friends and better relationships.
9. VISUALIZATION.	I see me as being friendly and being positive in a group of loving friends.
10. AFFIRMATION.	I look for the good and the beauty in people.
11. THE NEXT TIME THIS SITUATION COMES UP I WILL?	Next time I hear or think of a put down, I will say something positive about the person instead.

This Process: Bruno. Jealousy

1. RESENTMENT: the circumstance or situation: Jealous of wife.	Bruno speaks: I resent my wife talking to other men.
2. EFFECTS: Self-esteem, security, personal relationships, sex, ambition.	It affects my personal relationship with her. Our sex life grinds to a halt after I yell at her.
3. WHAT WAS MY PART IN IT? WHERE WAS I AT FAULT?	She was always pretty and friendly. The guys flocked around her. I yell at her to get her to stop talking to them.
4. FEELINGS: anger, fear, sad, shame, humiliation, guilt, pride, panic, depression, jealousy, indignation, inadequacy/failure, defiance apprehension, anguish, self-pity.	Anger at her for making me feel bad. Fear that she will run off with some other guy. Feeling inadequate that maybe I can't hold on to her.
5. NEGATIVE CHARACTERISTICS: fear, anger, pride, lust, sloth, envy, greed, selfish, dishonest, self-seeking, blame, victim, theft.	Anger. I get mad easily and blow my top. Fear that she'll leave me. Self-seeking: I want her to behave the way I want her to. Blame. It's all her fault that she makes me mad.
6. WHICH FEAR: loss of control, rejection, Inadequacy/failure, won't get something I want, will lose something I have.	Rejection and inadequacy. I'll lose something I have.

Chapter 6

The Release: Bruno

1. I SEE THAT ___ DID THE BEST ___ COULD GIVEN THE PLACE THAT ___ WAS IN.	Bruno: She does the best she can; she's naturally friendly and attractive.
2. DESCRIBE ___ POINT OF VIEW.	She thinks she's not doing anything wrong. Just because she talks to a guy, doesn't mean she'll jump into his arms.
3. LIST THE GOOD TRAITS THIS PERSON OR INSTITUTION HAD.	She is so beautiful, attractive and friendly. She is so much fun to be around.
4. I FREELY AND FULLY FORGIVE ___ TO THE BEST OF MY ABILITY.	I freely forgive her for being the way she is.
5. I CUT ___ LOOSE AND SET ___ FREE. NOW ___ IS FREE AND I AM FREE	I cut her free of my anger and remind myself that she is still my wife.
6. I BLESS (WISH GOOD FOR) ___.	I love her and wish the best for her, including a not so grumpy husband (me).
7. I APOLOGIZE FOR THE PAIN I CAUSED.	I'm sorry I caused her to feel bad when I yelled at her.
8. THE GIFT or THE LESSON I LEARNED WAS:	She is a different person who lives her life as she sees fit.
9. VISUALIZATION.	I see her coming toward me smiling with her arms stretched out.
10. AFFIRMATION.	I am good looking and lovable.
11. THE NEXT TIME THIS SITUATION COMES UP I WILL:	I will enjoy her attractiveness and that she is going home with me.

The Process: Sandra. Womanizer

1. RESENTMENT: The circumstance or situation: ANGER AT UNFAITHFUL LOVER.	Sandra speaks: I resent Chuck because he used me as one of his stable of "playmates" and would not make a commitment to an exclusive relationship.
2. EFFECTS: Self-esteem, security, personal relationships, sex, ambition.	This affects my self-esteem; I question whether I am a desirable woman. It affects my sex relations since we are no longer together.
3. WHAT WAS MY PART IN IT? WHERE WAS I AT FAULT?	I ignored the obvious warning signs, nor did I listen to family and friends who pointed out his interest in other women.
4. FEELINGS: anger, fear, sad, shame, humiliation, guilt, pride, panic, depression, jealousy, indignation, inadequacy/failure, defiance, apprehension, anguish, self-pity.	I am furious at him for not being the man I wanted him to be. I'm afraid I won't have another intense love in my life. I am ashamed that I let him get by with his behavior. I am humiliated that others will think how stupid I was. I am jealous that other women also appealed to him. I felt inadequate that I was not all he ever wanted in a woman. I was not enough. I fear I might fall for the same type of guy.
5. NEGATIVE CHARACTERISTICS: fear, anger, pride, lust, sloth, envy, greed, selfish, dishonest, blame, victim, theft.	Anger at him. Lust was a great motivator to continue the relationship. Envy/jealousy of the other women. Blame: I blame him for not being a trustworthy person. I felt I was a victim.
6. WHICH FEAR: loss of control, rejection, inadequacy/failure, won't get something I want, will lose something I have.	Rejection is big because he preferred other women. I didn't get something I wanted. Failure: I failed to hold him exclusively.

Chapter 6

The Release: Sandra

1. I SEE THAT ___ DID THE BEST ___ COULD GIVEN THE PLACE THAT ___ WAS IN.	Sandra: I see that Chuck did the best he could, given his belief that women were objects for his pleasure.
2. DESCRIBE ___ POINT OF VIEW.	He believed that women would fill his every want no matter what he asked.
3. LIST THE GOOD TRAITS THIS PERSON OR INSTITUTION HAD.	He was so attractive and good looking I felt like a million bucks just to be seen with him. He was a good conversationalist and a great lover.
4. I FREELY AND FULLY FORGIVE ___ TO THE BEST OF MY ABILITY.	I forgive him for being who he is.
5. I CUT ___ LOOSE AND SET ___ FREE. NOW ___ IS FREE AND I AM FREE.	I cut him loose and I am free.
6. I BLESS (WISH GOOD FOR) ___.	I wish for Chuck all things I want for myself: well-being, good health, happiness, and true love.
7. I APOLOGIZE FOR THE PAIN I CAUSED.	I'm sorry for the pain I caused when we broke up.
8. THE GIFT or THE LESSON I LEARNED WAS:	Listen but watch a person's behavior. Before deciding this is someone I can trust, I will seek others' opinions.
9. VISUALIZATION.	I am relieved of my obsession with anger and jealousy and can go on with my own life of many blessings, successes, and a healthy love.
10. AFFIRMATION.	I'm in the flow. I accept all good things life brings me.
11. THE NEXT TIME THIS SITUATION COMES UP I WILL:	I will build a friendship first. Let love come more slowly. No sex for 90 days.

The Process: Jim. Molested and Abused

Note: Jim used some other techniques as well to heal. I have included them so that you can know about different approaches.

1. I RESENT Mom BECAUSE:
   She sexually molested and physically abused me. Starting at age 4, she practiced oral copulation and threatened to bite off my penis if I told anyone. She stuck wooden sticks up my butt as I lay on the floor; she laughed and told me not to remove them. She put a knife through my tongue and twice at age 4 and 7 she tried to murder me by suffocation. Years later, when a chiropractor x-rayed my body he found evidence of dozens of broken bones on my arms and legs. She threatened me so that I could not tell Dad about the pain.

2. EFFECTS: Self-esteem, security, personal relationships sex relations:
   My self-esteem was affected tremendously. I didn't know why I deserved this treatment. I was numb to personal and sexual relationships for years. I was very insecure; no sense of being protected and absolutely powerless to protect myself.

3. *WHAT WAS MY PART IN IT? WHERE WAS I AT FAULT?*
   I was too afraid to tell anyone what was happening. My older sister and I went to Dad to ask him to get help for her. He said, "Nobody needs help if they have a strong mind, and she has a strong mind." As an adult, I told my dad what had happened, he did not acknowledge or say anything.

4. *FEELINGS: anger, fear, sad, shame, humiliation, guilt, pride, panic, depression, jealousy, indignation, inadequate/failure, defiance, apprehension, anguish, self-pity.*
   My feelings were shame, guilt, tremendous fear, deep sadness, unexpressed rage, victimized, helpless when faced with bullying or picked on, remorse, no control, unsafe, terrorized, depression. I could not feel or express anger when appropriate. I could feel rage but not being aware of the cause. I was frequently suicidal.

5. *NEGATIVE CHARACTERISTICS: fear, anger, pride, lust, sloth, envy, greed, selfish, dishonest, self-seeking, blame, victim, theft.*

Fear, anger, victim were the main ones as well as mistrust.

6. *WHICH FEAR: loss of control, rejection, inadequacy/failure, won't get something I want, or will lose something I have.*
Rejection, inadequacy, failure, will lose something I have (my penis) and loss of control were all at play in my life until I was healed.

The Release: Jim

1. *I SEE THAT* Mom *DID THE BEST SHE COULD GIVEN THE PLACE THAT SHE WAS IN.*
   She told me that her mother had been married nine times and that half of these stepfathers had molested her. I know that this behavior is passed on from generation to generation.

2. *DESCRIBE THEIR POINT OF VIEW.*
   Mom thought because this was done to her, that she could do it; it must have been okay since no one stopped it from happening for her.

   She was physically beautiful but with no self-worth. She did not love Dad. In fact, she fell in love with someone else before she was married but married Dad anyway. With her victim mentality, she could not give herself the good things in life; she felt she didn't deserve them. She was also afraid of being abandoned.

3. *LIST THE GOOD TRAITS THIS PERSON OR INSTITUTION HAD.*
   She was very beautiful and kept up her appearance. She was also a good cook and housekeeper.

4. *I FREELY AND FULLY FORGIVE* Mom *TO THE BEST OF MY ABILITY.*
   I worked on forgiveness for two decades in little increments. I rationalize that she was insane. Seeking spiritual deliverance, I prayed. I gave it to God and I worked with therapists. It was under hypnosis that I was able to have a conversation with Mom and me as a little boy. I could feel inside her mind. She felt deep, deep regret, sadness, remorse, guilt, shame even while she was abusing me. She said, "I wish I was dead." I was able to feel her torment and able to bless her. During that same hypnotic session, I got inside the little boy's head and felt his feelings; his hurt, rage, shame, remorse, hatred, powerlessness, and no control over his safely.

   I went to a Native American Shaman who performed rituals that took me back to the spirit world where I had a conversation with Mom. When we were in the spirit world before I was born, my soul begged her soul to be the perpetrator in this lifetime. Both she and my dad did not want to do this but out of their great love for me, they agreed.

For many years, I have studied "A Course in Miracles" and found much peace and forgiveness there.

5. *I CUT* both of them, Mom and Dad *LOOSE AND SET THEM FREE. NOW THEY ARE FREE AND I AM FREE.*

6. *I APOLOGIZE FOR THE PAIN I MAY HAVE CAUSED THEM*
   I did not feel the need to apologize except on the soul level for asking them to participate in something their souls did not want to do.

7. *I BLESS (WISH GOOD FOR) ___.*
   For both of them. I bless both of them absolutely. I can't wait to meet them back in the spirit world to tell them "Thank you" and "I love you" for the Gift I received.

8. *THE GIFT OR THE LESSON I LEARNED WAS:*
   I did not become a child molester or abuser so I feel that ending this behavior in my generation was what my soul needed to do. I have been able to build a deep trusting relationship with my daughters.
   I have learned to live from my heart, not from my ego. With all the psychological and spiritual work, I have come to understand others and myself. I've moved along my spiritual path understanding perception vs. projection, what allowing means, trusting everything, knowing what surrender is, knowing how to heal, and how to extend love.
   Even if called a stupid ass, I do not feel the need to defend or retaliate. Whatever is that person's stuff, it is his, not mine.

9. *VISUALIZATION:* I did not use this.

10. *AFFIRMATION:* I am now happy, joyous and free.

11. *THE NEXT TIME THIS SITUATION COMES UP I WILL:* I have no need to defend myself. If there is an abuser, I can set boundaries such as saying, "That is inappropriate and unacceptable".

The Process: Tom Puetz. Vietnam War

RESENTMENT: The circumstance or situation: *ANGER AT BEING DRAFTED.*	Tom Puetz speaks. I resented being drafted and sent to Vietnam. I also resented the "welcome home" we received with the put-downs and name-calling.
EFFECTS: self-esteem, security, personal relationships, sex, ambition.	Security: My dreams were put on hold as I went off to do my duty. Personal relationships: To be so completely misunderstood when I was defending these citizens and their freedom of speech – their right to call me a murderer.
WHAT WAS YOUR PART IN IT? WHERE WAS I AT FAULT?	This was my responsibility as a citizen; I had to participate in defending my country from communism.
FEELINGS: anger, fear, sad, shame, humiliation, guilt, pride, panic, depression, jealousy, indignation, inadequate/failure, defiance apprehension, anguish	Anger, fear, sadness, guilt, panic, depression, indignation, apprehension, defiance, and anguish
NEGATIVE CHARACTERISTICS: fear, anger, pride, lust, sloth, envy, greed, selfish, dishonest, self-seeking, blame, victim, theft.	Fear and anger.
WHICH FEAR: loss of control, rejection, inadequacy/failure, won't get something I want, or will lose something I have.	Loss of Control, banishment (rejection), fear of mutilation, fear of death, pain from a beating. Won't get out of this whole and alive (will lose something I have). The rejection from the anti-war group.

Chapter 6

THE RELEASE Tom Puetz

1. *I SEE THAT* America and the Military *DID THE BEST THEY COULD GIVEN THE PLACE THAT THEY WERE IN.* Many times they and I did not do the best we could. It was called making a mistake: not living up to your own rules.

2. *DESCRIBE THEIR POINT OF VIEW:* The government believed that Chinese communism would take over the rest of Southeast Asia that would strengthen China's goal of world domination.

3. *LIST THE GOOD TRAITS THIS PERSON OR INSTITUTION HAD.* The U.S. Military has done a great job keeping us free from enemies. I love this country and its deep values of freedom and opportunity.

4. *I FREELY AND FULLY FORGIVE _ America and the Military ____ TO THE BEST OF MY ABILITY.* Forgiveness is a process not something I did or do. Somewhere in that process I realized if I was going to forgive someone, I must have blamed them for something already. I judged them severely. Forgiveness implied judgment, wrongdoing, culpability. So no, I never freely and fully forgave. I came to the realization there was nothing to forgive. There was no blame only responsibility, no victim, or perpetrator only participants.

5. *I CUT THEM LOOSE AND SET THEM FREE. NOW THEY ARE FREE AND I AM FREE.* Yes, this feels good.

6. *I APOLOGIZE FOR THE PAIN I MAY HAVE CAUSED THEM.* Yes, this feels good.

7. *I BLESS (WISH GOOD FOR) THEM.* Yes, this feels good. I suppose we can heal ourselves but it is much more effective if the community (the village) takes part. To know that I was hurt and that my suffering was recognized was very important .The acknowledgement does not have to come from the perpetrator, it would have felt better coming from the people of this country.

8. *THE GIFT OR THE LESSON I LEARNED WAS: there* are no perpetrators or victims only participants. A major contribution to my healing was participation in a world peace stance. I was part of a performance done with four masked dancers. I read a poem and the dancers performed a ritual healing.

    Here is a copy of the poem.

BATTLE RAGE

This rage – I can't really measure, goes on forever.
Can't contain it, can't make it stop, and can't see the end.
This fugitive sample of combat survival
Can't be buried, I am always harried by…

This rage — kept growing when you said, "Welcome home".
Instead of, "We didn't know the death of tenderness,
The killing, the price paid, and …

This Rage – Is a partition held in place by my lack of contrition:
A division risen on backs turned, eyes averted;
A wall, polished and black, with no shelf to receive retribution.
No portal that understanding passes, only the reflection of…

This Rage —you won't accept in me, a soldier
You sent to hold your honor in sacred trust,
And so disguised the violence as valor.
You reveled in my bravery now demand I hide my frailty, and

This Rage
by © Tom Puetz

9. *VISUALIZATION:* I could see myself being held and comforted.

10. *AFFIRMATION:* The song, "Let There Be Peace On Earth And Let It Begin With Me."

11. *THE NEXT TIME THIS SITUATION COMES UP I WILL:* Do whatever I can to avoid sending troops to war.

Chapter 7
Conclusion

"The distance doesn't matter; it is only the
first step that is difficult."
Madame du Deffand

Congratulations. You have done so much work on yourself that you deserve a reward. And you got it. You have advanced along the path of freeing yourself of the negativity that you have carried with you all these years. Your soul is that much freer and your cardio-vascular system will thank you for not flooding it with that damaging cortisol.

Your relationships will thank you for accepting them as they are – yes, with all their tarnishes and blemishes. That's the way they are and that's the way you are.

In the 12 step programs, there is another step; that is to share your inventory with another person. Usually a wise choice is a sponsor, minister, counselor, psychologist, or other professional. Not only do they keep what they hear confidential, but they also know how to listen without judging. Family members or close relationships are not good choices – later they may throw something back at you that you shared in confidence.

May your continued journey be filled with love, joy, and true happiness. May you find your own joyous elf who sings sweet songs to please yourself.

Namaste.

Bibliography

Alcoholics Anonymous World Services. *"The Twelve Steps and Twelve Traditions."* New York. 1981.

Cohen, Alan. "A Deep Breath of Life". Hay House. Carlsbad, CA. 1996.

Dyer, Wayne. *"The Power of Intention."* DVD. Hay House. Carlsbad, CA. 2003.

Falco, Howard. "*I am: The Power of Discovering Who You Really Are."* Jeremy T Tarcher/Penguin. New York. 2010.

"*Fourth-Step Workshop Lectures."* Phyllis G. San Diego, CA.

Puetz, Tom. "*Secret Choices."* Dragon Tales Books. Sedona, AZ. 2014

"*Renaissance."* In *Collected Lyrics.* Edna St. Vincent Millay. Washington Square Press. New York. 1966.

The Twelve Steps of Alcoholics Anonymous

1. We admitted that we were powerless over alcohol – that our lives had become unmanageable.

2. Came to believe that a Power greater than ourselves could restore us to sanity.

3. Made a decision to turn our will and our lives over to the care of God, <u>as we understood Him.</u>

4. Made a searching and fearless moral inventory of ourselves.

5. Admitted to God, to ourselves, and to another human being the exact nature of our wrongs.

6. We were entirely ready to have God remove all these defects of character.

7. Humbly asked Him to remove our shortcomings.

8. Made a list of all persons we had harmed and became willing to make amends to them all.

9. Made direct amends to such people wherever possible, except when to do so would injure them or others

10. Continued to take personal inventory, and when we were wrong promptly admitted it.

11. Sought through prayer and meditation to improve our conscious contact with God,<u> as we understood Him,</u> praying only for knowledge of His will for us, and the power to carry it out.

12. Having had a spiritual awakening as the result of these steps, we tried to carry this message to other alcoholics and to practice these principles in all our affairs.

WORKSHEETS
There are two styles of worksheets; choose the one you're most comfortable with.

© Molly Nelson

THE PROCESS NARRATIVE STYLE

1. I RESENT _____ BECAUSE: The circumstance or situation.

2. EFFECTS: Self-esteem, security, personal relationships, sex.

3. WHAT WAS MY PART IN IT? WHERE WAS I AT FAULT?

4. FEELINGS: anger, fear, sad, shame, humiliation, guilt, pride, panic, depression, jealousy, indignation, inadequate/failure, defiance, apprehension, anguish, self-pity.

5. NEGATIVE CHARACTERISTICS: fear, anger, pride, lust, sloth, envy, greed, selfish, dishonest, self-seeking, blame, victim, theft.

6. WHICH FEAR: loss of control, rejection, inadequacy/failure, won't get something I want, will lose something I have.

© Molly Nelson

THE RELEASE NARRATIVE STYLE

1. I SEE THAT _____ DID THE BEST _____ COULD GIVEN THE PLACE THAT _____ WAS/WERE IN.

2. DESCRIBE THEIR POINT OF VIEW.

3. LIST THE GOOD TRAITS THIS PERSON OR INSTITUTION HAD.

4. I FREELY AND FULLY FORGIVE _____ TO THE BEST OF MY ABILITY.

5. I CUT _____ LOOSE AND SET _____ FREE. NOW THEY ARE FREE AND I AM FREE.

6. I APOLOGIZE FOR THE PAIN I MAY HAVE CAUSED.

7. I BLESS (WISH GOOD FOR) _____.

8. THE GIFT OR THE LESSON I LEARNED WAS:

9. VISUALIZATION.

10. AFFIRMATION.

11. THE NEXT TIME THIS SITUATION COMES UP I WILL:

© Molly Nelson

THE PROCESS CHART STYLE

1. RESENTMENT: The circumstance or situation.	
2. EFFECTS: self-esteem, security, personal relationships, sex, ambition.	
3. WHAT WAS MY PART IN IT? WHERE WAS I AT FAULT?	
4. FEELINGS: anger, fear, sad, shame, humiliation, guilt, pride, panic, depression, jealousy, indignation, inadequate/failure, defiance, apprehension, anguish, self-pity.	
5. NEGATIVE CHARACTERISTICS: fear, anger, pride, lust, sloth, envy, greed, selfish, dishonest, self-seeking, blame, victim, theft.	
6. WHICH FEAR: loss of control, rejection, inadequacy/failure, won't get something I want, will lose something I have.	

© Molly Nelson

THE RELEASE CHART STYLE

1. I SEE THAT ___ DID THE BEST ___ COULD GIVEN THE PLACE THAT ___ WAS IN.	
2. DESCRIBE ___ POINT OF VIEW.	
3. LIST THE GOOD TRAITS THIS PERSON OR INSTITUTION HAD.	
4. I FREELY AND FULLY FORGIVE ___ TO THE BEST OF MY ABILITY.	
5. I CUT ___ LOOSE AND SET ___ FREE. NOW ___ IS FREE AND I AM FREE.	
6. I BLESS (WISH GOOD FOR) ___.	
7. I APOLOGIZE FOR THE PAIN I CAUSED.	
8. THE GIFT or THE LESSON I LEARNED WAS:	
9. VISUALIZATION.	
10. AFFIRMATION.	
11. WHAT I WILL DO THE NEXT TIME THIS HAPPENS	

© Molly Nelson

THE PROCESS NARRATIVE STYLE

1. I RESENT _____ BECAUSE: The circumstance or situation.

2. EFFECTS: Self-esteem, security, personal relationships, sex.

3. WHAT WAS MY PART IN IT? WHERE WAS I AT FAULT?

4. FEELINGS: anger, fear, sad, shame, humiliation, guilt, pride, panic, depression, jealousy, indignation, inadequate/failure, defiance, apprehension, anguish, self-pity.

5. NEGATIVE CHARACTERISTICS: fear, anger, pride, lust, sloth, envy, greed, selfish, dishonest, self-seeking, blame, victim, theft.

6. WHICH FEAR: loss of control, rejection, inadequacy/failure, won't get something I want, will lose something I have.

© Molly Nelson

THE RELEASE NARRATIVE STYLE

1. I SEE THAT _____ DID THE BEST _____ COULD GIVEN THE PLACE THAT _____ WAS/WERE IN.

2. DESCRIBE THEIR POINT OF VIEW.

3. LIST THE GOOD TRAITS THIS PERSON OR INSTITUTION HAD.

4. I FREELY AND FULLY FORGIVE _____ TO THE BEST OF MY ABILITY.

5. I CUT _____ LOOSE AND SET _____ FREE. NOW THEY ARE FREE AND I AM FREE.

6. I APOLOGIZE FOR THE PAIN I MAY HAVE CAUSED.

7. I BLESS (WISH GOOD FOR) _____.

8. THE GIFT OR THE LESSON I LEARNED WAS:

9. VISUALIZATION.

10. AFFIRMATION.

11. THE NEXT TIME THIS SITUATION COMES UP I WILL:

© Molly Nelson

THE PROCESS CHART STYLE

1. RESENTMENT: The circumstance or situation.	
2. EFFECTS: self-esteem, security, personal relationships, sex, ambition.	
3. WHAT WAS MY PART IN IT? WHERE WAS I AT FAULT?	
4. FEELINGS: anger, fear, sad, shame, humiliation, guilt, pride, panic, depression, jealousy, indignation, inadequate/failure, defiance, apprehension, anguish, self-pity.	
5. NEGATIVE CHARACTERISTICS: fear, anger, pride, lust, sloth, envy, greed, selfish, dishonest, self-seeking, blame, victim, theft.	
6. WHICH FEAR: loss of control, rejection, inadequacy/failure, won't get something I want, will lose something I have.	

© Molly Nelson

THE RELEASE CHART STYLE

1. I SEE THAT ___ DID THE BEST ___ COULD GIVEN THE PLACE THAT ___ WAS IN.	
2. DESCRIBE ___ POINT OF VIEW.	
3. LIST THE GOOD TRAITS THIS PERSON OR INSTITUTION HAD.	
4. I FREELY AND FULLY FORGIVE ___ TO THE BEST OF MY ABILITY.	
5. I CUT ___ LOOSE AND SET ___ FREE. NOW ___ IS FREE AND I AM FREE.	
6. I BLESS (WISH GOOD FOR) ___.	
7. I APOLOGIZE FOR THE PAIN I CAUSED.	
8. THE GIFT or THE LESSON I LEARNED WAS:	
9. VISUALIZATION.	
10. AFFIRMATION.	
11. WHAT I WILL DO THE NEXT TIME THIS HAPPENS	

© Molly Nelson

THE PROCESS NARRATIVE STYLE

1. I RESENT _____ BECAUSE: The circumstance or situation.

2. EFFECTS: Self-esteem, security, personal relationships, sex.

3. WHAT WAS MY PART IN IT? WHERE WAS I AT FAULT?

4. FEELINGS: anger, fear, sad, shame, humiliation, guilt, pride, panic, depression, jealousy, indignation, inadequate/failure, defiance, apprehension, anguish, self-pity.

5. NEGATIVE CHARACTERISTICS: fear, anger, pride, lust, sloth, envy, greed, selfish, dishonest, self-seeking, blame, victim, theft.

6. WHICH FEAR: loss of control, rejection, inadequacy/failure, won't get something I want, will lose something I have.

© Molly Nelson

THE RELEASE NARRATIVE STYLE

1. I SEE THAT _____ DID THE BEST _____ COULD GIVEN THE PLACE THAT _____ WAS/WERE IN.

2. *DESCRIBE THEIR POINT OF VIEW.*

3. *LIST THE GOOD TRAITS THIS PERSON OR INSTITUTION HAD.*

4. *I FREELY AND FULLY FORGIVE _____ TO THE BEST OF MY ABILITY.*

5. *I CUT _____ LOOSE AND SET _____ FREE. NOW THEY ARE FREE AND I AM FREE.*

6. *I APOLOGIZE FOR THE PAIN I MAY HAVE CAUSED.*

7. *I BLESS (WISH GOOD FOR) _____.*

8. *THE GIFT OR THE LESSON I LEARNED WAS:*

9. *VISUALIZATION.*

10. *AFFIRMATION.*

11. *THE NEXT TIME THIS SITUATION COMES UP I WILL:*

© Molly Nelson

THE PROCESS CHART STYLE

1. RESENTMENT: The circumstance or situation.	
2. EFFECTS: self-esteem, security, personal relationships, sex, ambition.	
3. WHAT WAS MY PART IN IT? WHERE WAS I AT FAULT?	
4. FEELINGS: anger, fear, sad, shame, humiliation, guilt, pride, panic, depression, jealousy, indignation, inadequate/failure, defiance, apprehension, anguish, self-pity.	
5. NEGATIVE CHARACTERISTICS: fear, anger, pride, lust, sloth, envy, greed, selfish, dishonest, self-seeking, blame, victim, theft.	
6. WHICH FEAR: loss of control, rejection, inadequacy/failure, won't get something I want, will lose something I have.	

© Molly Nelson

THE RELEASE CHART STYLE

1. I SEE THAT ___ DID THE BEST ___ COULD GIVEN THE PLACE THAT ___ WAS IN.	
2. DESCRIBE ___ POINT OF VIEW.	
3. LIST THE GOOD TRAITS THIS PERSON OR INSTITUTION HAD.	
4. I FREELY AND FULLY FORGIVE ___ TO THE BEST OF MY ABILITY.	
5. I CUT ___ LOOSE AND SET ___ FREE. NOW ___ IS FREE AND I AM FREE.	
6. I BLESS (WISH GOOD FOR) ___.	
7. I APOLOGIZE FOR THE PAIN I CAUSED.	
8. THE GIFT or THE LESSON I LEARNED WAS:	
9. VISUALIZATION.	
10. AFFIRMATION.	
11. WHAT I WILL DO THE NEXT TIME THIS HAPPENS	

© Molly Nelson

THE PROCESS NARRATIVE STYLE

1. I RESENT _____ BECAUSE: The circumstance or situation.

2. EFFECTS: Self-esteem, security, personal relationships, sex.

3. WHAT WAS MY PART IN IT? WHERE WAS I AT FAULT?

4. FEELINGS: anger, fear, sad, shame, humiliation, guilt, pride, panic, depression, jealousy, indignation, inadequate/failure, defiance, apprehension, anguish, self-pity.

5. NEGATIVE CHARACTERISTICS: fear, anger, pride, lust, sloth, envy, greed, selfish, dishonest, self-seeking, blame, victim, theft.

6. WHICH FEAR: loss of control, rejection, inadequacy/failure, won't get something I want, will lose something I have.

© Molly Nelson

THE RELEASE NARRATIVE STYLE

1. I SEE THAT _____ DID THE BEST _____ COULD GIVEN THE PLACE THAT _____ WAS/WERE IN.

2. *DESCRIBE THEIR POINT OF VIEW.*

3. *LIST THE GOOD TRAITS THIS PERSON OR INSTITUTION HAD.*

4. *I FREELY AND FULLY FORGIVE _____ TO THE BEST OF MY ABILITY.*

5. *I CUT _____ LOOSE AND SET _____ FREE. NOW THEY ARE FREE AND I AM FREE.*

6. *I APOLOGIZE FOR THE PAIN I MAY HAVE CAUSED.*

7. *I BLESS (WISH GOOD FOR) _____.*

8. *THE GIFT OR THE LESSON I LEARNED WAS:*

9. *VISUALIZATION.*

10. *AFFIRMATION.*

11. *THE NEXT TIME THIS SITUATION COMES UP I WILL:*

© Molly Nelson

THE PROCESS CHART STYLE

1. RESENTMENT: The circumstance or situation.	
2. EFFECTS: self-esteem, security, personal relationships, sex, ambition.	
3. WHAT WAS MY PART IN IT? WHERE WAS I AT FAULT?	
4. FEELINGS: anger, fear, sad, shame, humiliation, guilt, pride, panic, depression, jealousy, indignation, inadequate/failure, defiance, apprehension, anguish, self-pity.	
5. NEGATIVE CHARACTERISTICS: fear, anger, pride, lust, sloth, envy, greed, selfish, dishonest, self-seeking, blame, victim, theft.	
6. WHICH FEAR: loss of control, rejection, inadequacy/failure, won't get something I want, will lose something I have.	

© Molly Nelson

THE RELEASE CHART STYLE

1. I SEE THAT ___ DID THE BEST ___ COULD GIVEN THE PLACE THAT ___ WAS IN.	
2. DESCRIBE ___ POINT OF VIEW.	
3. LIST THE GOOD TRAITS THIS PERSON OR INSTITUTION HAD.	
4. I FREELY AND FULLY FORGIVE ___ TO THE BEST OF MY ABILITY.	
5. I CUT ___ LOOSE AND SET ___ FREE. NOW ___ IS FREE AND I AM FREE.	
6. I BLESS (WISH GOOD FOR) ___.	
7. I APOLOGIZE FOR THE PAIN I CAUSED.	
8. THE GIFT or THE LESSON I LEARNED WAS:	
9. VISUALIZATION.	
10. AFFIRMATION.	
11. WHAT I WILL DO THE NEXT TIME THIS HAPPENS	

© Molly Nelson

Made in the USA
Middletown, DE
13 October 2023